What Is

Gaming

Disorder?

By Tammy Gagne

ReferencePoint
Press®

San Diego, CA

Content Consultant: Christopher Ferguson, Professor of Psychology, Stetson University

LIBRARY OF CONGRESS CATALOGING-IN-PUBLICATION DATA

Names: Gagne, Tammy, author.
Title: What is gaming disorder? / by Tammy Gagne.
Description: San Diego, CA : ReferencePoint Press, [2021] | Series: Teen disorders | Includes bibliographical references and index. | Audience: Grades 10-12
Identifiers: LCCN 2020003545 (print) | LCCN 2020003546 (eBook) | ISBN 9781682829530 (hardcover) | ISBN 9781682829547 (eBook)
Subjects: LCSH: Internet games--Psychological aspects. | Video game addiction--Treatment.
Classification: LCC RC569.5.V53 G34 2021 (print) | LCC RC569.5.V53 (eBook) | DDC 616.85/84--dc23
LC record available at https://lccn.loc.gov/2020003545
LC eBook record available at https://lccn.loc.gov/2020003546

CONTENTS

When Gaming Gets Out of Control

Jamie Callis has fond memories of his introduction to video games. When he was about four or five years old, he would sit in his father's lap while his father played. It doesn't take young kids long to learn how video games work—and how to win at them. Although their hand-to-eye coordination is still being developed, children can be impressively adept at maneuvering the controls. The bright colors and engaging sounds form an inviting world that beckons young players to keep playing.

Soon, Jamie had advanced to playing video games independently. He was already playing games such as *Halo* and *Call of Duty* by the time he was seven. By thirteen, gaming had changed from just a fun pastime to a habit. "I was playing a game called *RuneScape* for upwards of 16 hours a day," he confided to news website Wales Online. "I just remember falling in love with it as there were so many skills involved."[1]

New technologies are becoming a part of our everyday lives. In 2019, an estimated 80 percent of teenagers owned some sort of gaming console.

He also fell in love with the escape that his video games

provided. In those virtual worlds, he found a second family of

sorts. He would chat privately with other players as they made their way through various quests. Gaming became his main source of socialization. "It was difficult," he said. "I kind of had no friends. I wasn't close with my family."[2] He even let his grades slip as a result of all the time he spent gaming.

"My entire teenage years were taken up with my family being constantly concerned about me," he recalled, "but I didn't really see it as an issue until I was 16 or 17."[3] Finally, a week before his nineteenth birthday, Jamie decided to quit gaming. Knowing he had a problem, but not knowing another way to deal with it, he chose to remove gaming from his life both suddenly and completely. Like many people who give up habits abruptly, he called it "going cold turkey."[4]

Giving up the games with so little preparation—and so little understanding of his addiction to them—sent Jamie into a devastating depression. Fortunately, he was able to deal with both problems with the help of a college counselor. At twenty-one, Jamie reported that gaming was no longer a problem for him. He was spending his recreation time hanging out with real-world friends, going to the movies, and traveling.

There are therapies that can help treat video game addiction. A therapist helps shift thoughts and behaviors about gaming and promote a healthier lifestyle.

He would never forget the hold that games once had over him, though. His experience left him with a profound awareness of how a seemingly innocent pastime can transform into a disorder.

Video games such as *Fortnite* have become popular all over the world. But some experts warn that games like this can be dangerous when played too much.

For many years no name existed for the type of problem Jamie had dealt with. Today, however, many mental health professionals call it gaming disorder. Its causes, symptoms, and treatment—and even its existence as a psychological disorder—are still being debated. Psychologist Jonathan D.

Raskin explained in a 2019 article for *Psychology Today*, "Those who firmly believe in gaming addiction contend that there is ample research evidence that people can become addicted to behaviors just as they can become addicted to drugs."[5] However, psychiatrist Meredith Gansner noted the same year in an article for *Psychiatric Times*, "Gaming disorder seems to be a fitting diagnosis, but its existence as an independent mental health condition remains highly controversial, with many researchers and clinicians divided on this issue."[6] Whether gaming is a cause of problems or a symptom of underlying mental illness, it's definitely an issue worth taking a look at.

CHAPTER ONE

What Is Gaming Disorder?

P laying video games—whether on television game consoles, computers, or handheld devices—is a common pastime among young people. In 2018, the video game industry collected more than $100 billion in worldwide sales, and market data suggests that this gargantuan figure will only grow over time. Video games offer a myriad of benefits to the kids who play them. They help develop visual-spatial skills, increase problem-solving abilities, and can even lead to stronger social connections, especially when real-life friends share an interest in a particular game. Despite all these advantages, video games are associated with mental health difficulties for some players, though it is not clear whether games cause these problems or some youth turn to games when they are stressed or sad.

Ninety percent of American kids ages thirteen to seventeen play video games. For boys the number is even higher, at

Video games have become a huge industry. They represent an enormous share of the overall money that people spend on entertainment.

97 percent. More than half of these teens spend an average of at least 2.5 hours a day enmeshed in these electronic worlds. A small number of kids and young adults greatly overdo gaming. In rare cases, they even forsake nearly all other activities in their

lives for this one form of entertainment. This problem leads many people to ask exactly how much video game time is too much. In its guidelines, the American Academy of Pediatrics does not set a time limit for teens. Rather, it notes that screen time should be balanced with schoolwork, socialization time, exercise, and adequate sleep. Screen time is an umbrella term for time spent watching television, playing video games, or taking part in any other pastime that involves a screen. Spending too much time gaming can prevent young people from taking part in other important activities, such as exercise and socialization, but even scientists who have conducted clinical research on this topic have not been able to pinpoint the exact amount of time that constitutes too much. In an article for HealthyPlace, mental health counselor Tanya J. Peterson wrote, "The most definitive answer is that there isn't yet a clear recommendation for the maximum number of hours kids should spend playing video games and generally using 'screens.'"[7] Some studies suggest that youth can get away with nearly five to six hours per day before noticing any level of impairment.

As experts attempt to determine the exact amount of time that crosses the line from a pastime to a problem, mental health professionals encourage video game enthusiasts to consider whether their game time encroaches upon other, more important activities in their lives. For example, playing video games for

THE GAMING INDUSTRY

In 2018, the gaming industry took in more revenue than other popular entertainment industries, including television, movies, and digital music.

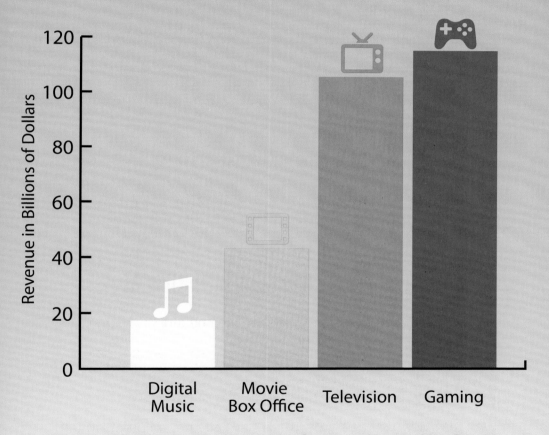

Angelo M. D'Argenio, "Statistically, Video Games Are Now the Most Popular and Profitable Form of Entertainment," GameCrate, July 10, 2018. www.gamecrate.com.

more than five hours each day could possibly interfere with a young person's ability to get enough sleep, engage in physical activity, and dedicate time to homework. Gamers who are prioritizing their game time above these important tasks could have a problem.

Gaming disorder is the clinical term for this problem. A person with this disorder has a lack of control over his or her gaming habits. While family members and friends might joke that a person has become "addicted" to gaming, when gaming is overdone experts tend to use the term *pathological gaming* to avoid making the condition sound too much like substance abuse. Most people who experience gaming disorder symptoms are able to go back to normal gaming without professional treatment, but a small number cannot.

PLAYERS MOST LIKELY TO EXHIBIT PATHOLOGICAL GAMING SYMPTOMS

Certain groups are more likely to experience pathological gaming than others. Young male gamers face the highest risk of experiencing pathological gaming. Scans of the brains of men who play video games excessively have showed changes to the regions of the brain that control impulsivity.

Life circumstances also play a role in a person's risk for gaming disorder. As gaming writer Joseph Knoop stated in a

Balancing schoolwork and games can be challenging. This can put university students at a higher risk for unhealthy gaming.

2018 article for the Daily Dot, "University students, in particular, may be particularly susceptible to gaming addiction because they generally have more time on their hands, some expendable income, high-speed internet access, and may be struggling to adjust [to] life away from home."[8] Challenging life circumstances after college—such as stress at work, problems in romantic relationships, and family issues—can also pose an increased risk to gamers for developing gaming disorder.

One possibility is that pathological gaming is not caused by games, but people with preexisting mental health disorders turn to games in order to feel better when they are anxious or depressed. Some studies confirm that other mental health conditions come first and then lead to pathological gaming, but not the other way around. If this is true, pathological gaming might be better thought of as a red flag for mental illness, rather than a unique condition brought on by too much video game playing.

A 2017 study conducted in Canada, Germany, the United Kingdom, and the United States collected information from nearly 19,000 gamers. The majority of the participants, about 65 percent, did not struggle with pathological gaming at all. A small number of the gamers, less than 3 percent, reported experiencing at least five of the symptoms of the disorder. Psychology professors Patrick M. Markey of Villanova University and Christopher J. Ferguson of Stetson University are skeptical of gaming disorder as an independent condition. They found the data from this research illuminating. Writing about the study, they explained, "This important study suggests that video game addiction might be a real thing, but it is not the epidemic that some have made it out to be."[9]

> "This important study suggests that video game addiction might be a real thing, but it is not the epidemic that some have made it out to be."[9]
>
> —Psychology professors Patrick M. Markey and Christopher J. Ferguson

Some parents may worry that playing video games will hinder their teens' social development. A common misperception exists about gamers being loners, but Dr. Nick Taylor, an assistant professor of communication at North Carolina State University, dispelled this myth during a 2014 interview with CNET. "Gamers aren't the antisocial basement dwellers we see in pop culture stereotypes; they're highly social people. This won't be a surprise to the gaming community, but it's worth telling everyone else. Loners are outliers in gaming, not the norm."[10] Likewise, spending lots of time playing video games is just one factor in gaming disorder; simply being an avid gamer does not equate to having a disorder.

Young people who rely on gaming for the majority of their social interactions are more prone to developing gaming disorder, however. Some kids who do not find much social

Gamers may appear to be isolated when sitting alone with headphones. But they may be interacting with their friends in online games.

acceptance at school or in other real-life settings may turn

to online gaming communities to find others who share their

interests. Massively multiplayer online games, or MMOs, can be especially welcoming to these individuals. Some games allow players to create groups called guilds in which players can join together to work toward a common goal. Since these games are running at all times of the day, a player can amass a large circle of online friends and meet up with them in these virtual realms whenever they like. In a piece for the *Washington Post*, journalist Caitlin Gibson wrote, "Logging off is that much harder for kids who feel a very real bond to their online friends and teammates."[11]

Other evidence suggests that schools and parents can actually bring on gaming disorder. For instance, one long-term study of Korean kids found that stress caused by parents and schools tended to lead to overuse of games. However, the time spent on games itself wasn't as predictive of problems. This suggests that often the problems that lead to gaming disorder don't come from the games themselves but rather the person's social world, and the person turns to games to reduce stress.

> "Logging off is that much harder for kids who feel a very real bond to their online friends and teammates."[11]
>
> —*Journalist Caitlin Gibson*

HOW MANY PEOPLE SUFFER FROM GAMING DISORDER?

Many experts agree that only a small part of the population actually ends up developing gaming disorder. In 2017, a study that appeared in the *American Journal of Psychiatry* estimated the number to be just 1 percent or less of the worldwide population, but even this small percentage translates to about 75 million people. Other studies have found that the number is even higher. Some researchers claim that as many as 15 percent of teens suffer from this problem, though most scholars agree these numbers are unrealistic. Different figures arise because different studies define gaming disorder differently.

Many experts do not even think that gaming disorder is, in fact, a true disorder. The *Diagnostic and Statistical Manual of Mental Disorders (DSM)* is a handbook used to standardize diagnoses among mental health professionals. It lists gaming disorder as a "Condition for Further Study" in the handbook's most recent edition, the *DSM-5*, which was released in 2013.

Many doctors and laypeople alike also question the validity of the disorder, wondering whether considering it a unique mental illness is the best way of discussing pathological gaming. During a 2019 interview with *Psychiatry Advisor* on the topic, Ferguson pointed out that people can overdo many behaviors that aren't classified as addictions: "Is it something about video games that makes them different from shopping or exercise or food or sex or other things people can do excessively, or is it that individuals have difficulty regulating a fun thing?"[12]

Gaming disorder has only recently been classified as a disorder by the World Health Organization. Professionals disagree on the severity and prevalence of the disorder.

In 2018, the World Health Organization (WHO) added gaming disorder to its *International Classification of Diseases (ICD 11)* publication. The move prompted many discussions

Why the WHO's Classification Matters

The World Health Organization's addition of gaming disorder to its *International Classification of Diseases* (*ICD 11*) resulted in significant controversy. The WHO's decision was immediately opposed by the media and technology divisions of the American Psychological Association and the Psychological Society of Ireland, which contended that the diagnosis isn't based in science and may cause unintended harms. One of the things that mental health professionals need most to treat this issue effectively is to conduct more research about it. On one hand, people who suffer from the disorder will have an easier time getting their insurance companies to cover the cost of therapy for the problem. Without the classification, medical bills could be denied because of the lack of an official diagnosis. On the other hand, many people with gaming disorder have another diagnosis that insurance will cover. And critics contend an unscientific diagnosis could result in misdiagnosis, exposing patients to unproven, harmful treatments. For instance, boot camps in China that claim to treat gaming disorder have resulted in several deaths. The *DSM*'s move to describe the disorder as a "Condition for Further Study" could be helpful in accumulating more data.

on the subject because the WHO was the first major health authority to grant the problem status as a behavioral addiction. Some critics of the diagnosis see excessive gaming as a symptom of other mental health issues—such as anxiety, attention-deficit/hyperactivity disorder (ADHD), and depression—instead of as a mental health disorder of its own. They also point out that the dopamine released when a person plays video games is far less than a drug addict experiences. The drug methamphetamine, for example, causes the release of twelve times the dopamine of video game play.

Many people play video games without becoming addicted. Gaming disorder can only be diagnosed if playing video games begins to interfere with other aspects of life.

Psychologist Nicholas Kardaras thinks the gaming disorder diagnosis is warranted but many people are simply unwilling to face it. "We have, as a society, gone all-in on tech," he said during a 2019 interview on National Public Radio. "So we don't want some buzz-killing truth sayers telling us that the emperor has no clothes and that the devices that we've all so fallen in love with can be a problem."[13]

It is no secret that video games have become both a universal form of entertainment and a scapegoat for many of the problems in modern society. As Ferguson told the news website Vox in 2018, "Often times, there are these kinds of visceral, negative reactions to new technologies that in some cases lead to pretty extreme claims. It's not hard to see that in the video game addiction realm, where you see headlines that video games are 'digital heroin.'"[14]

Some people even see the gaming disorder diagnosis as unjustly calling out a certain group of people. *Orlando Sentinel* columnist Shannon Green thinks that gaming is being singled out when society is seeing many other behaviors, such as online shopping and cell phone use, being taken to extremes. "Frankly," she wrote in a 2019 piece for the newspaper, "this entire discussion reeks of cultural bias toward a younger generation that enjoys virtual entertainment."[15]

"Frankly, this entire discussion reeks of cultural bias toward a younger generation that enjoys virtual entertainment."[15]

—Orlando Sentinel *columnist Shannon Green*

Supporters of the diagnosis emphasize that merely playing video games, even to extremes, is not the only symptom of gaming disorder. They insist that in order to be diagnosed with the condition, a person must meet a list of criteria that includes several other factors. These factors are what define the condition as a true disorder.

CHAPTER TWO

How Is Gaming Disorder Diagnosed?

t is easy to assume that the cause of gaming disorder is simply too much time spent gaming, but the amount of time a person spends playing is only one part of a diagnosis. Many other factors are involved in this complicated problem. One of the biggest is how this time affects other parts of the gamer's life. People who spend most of their free time playing video games but also keep up with their other activities—from school or work to plans with family and friends—are unlikely to be suffering from gaming disorder. Those who postpone necessary activities such as sleeping or eating to carve out more game time more than just for the occasional marathon gaming session, or those who are often late to or absent from their routine commitments due to gaming, on the other hand, might have a problem.

Another factor that can impact a gaming disorder diagnosis is whether the gamer suffers from another mental health issue,

Those with gaming disorder are more likely to suffer from other mental health issues, such as depression. Video games provide a temporary escape, but ultimately they do not offer a permanent solution to underlying problems.

such as depression or ADHD. Often people who suffer from one of these problems, as well as spending large amounts of time in front of a video game screen, face an increased risk for developing gaming disorder.

Experts disagree about whether depression leads to gaming disorder or if it is, in fact, the other way around, but a connection between the two problems seems clear. More than

26 percent of the people who suffer from gaming disorder also have depression. By contrast, just 11 percent of people without gaming disorder suffer from depression.

Some young people who struggle with depression find solace in playing video games. On the surface this solace may seem like a positive coping mechanism. When these people experience negative thoughts and feelings, playing a game can help them escape that negativity, at least temporarily. When they use gaming to mask these symptoms of depression for too long, however, time spent gaming becomes another symptom. Gaming can also potentially worsen depression by decreasing the amount of exercise, nutrition, and in-person social interaction a gamer receives. Getting all of these things is important for people's health and well-being whether they suffer from depression or not; not getting them can even place a gamer at a greater risk of developing depression.

In 2018, researchers at Beijing Normal University released a study of 2,000 gamers between the ages of sixteen and twenty-one. Each one had spent more than four years gaming for at least two hours each day. After identifying 63 of these gamers as pathological gamers, the study then took a closer look at these individuals. The researchers stated, "Individuals cope with their emotional distress by playing internet games [but] prolonged internet gaming induces depression due to lack of, or withdrawal from, real-life relationships."[16] The study also found that greater depression at a younger age made individuals more prone to pathological gaming later in life.

Generally, evidence now suggests that most games are not more addictive than other behaviors people may overdo, such as shopping, exercise,

> "Individuals cope with their emotional distress by playing internet games [but] prolonged internet gaming induces depression due to lack of, or withdrawal from, real-life relationships."[16]
>
> —*Researchers at Beijing Normal University, 2018*

sex, or food. However, for people who already have problems regulating their behavior, some aspects of certain games may be an issue. For instance, people with gambling problems may spend more money on loot boxes (paid objects in a game that provide players with random in-game rewards) than people without gambling issues, although the amounts are small, a difference of about $20 to $40 a month. There isn't evidence loot boxes cause problematic gambling, however.

SYMPTOMS OF GAMING DISORDER

The symptoms of gaming disorder begin with a lack of control over time spent gaming. Players may genuinely try to spend less time gaming, but they might find it impossible to honor limits, even those they set for themselves. Many gamers, even those

Someone who suffers from gaming disorder may stay up late to play video games. The need for gaming is constant and takes place over other needs, such as eating, socializing, and sleeping.

without a problem, often say things such as "Just another five minutes" and end up playing slightly past this extended time period. But for those suffering from gaming disorder, five more minutes can easily turn into five more hours. It is the lack of control more than the time itself that signals the problem.

Alok Kanojia is now a psychiatrist who treats people with gaming disorder, but as a younger person, he suffered from gaming disorder himself. His own experience has given him unique insight as a caregiver. "I basically had less than a 2.0 GPA after two years of college because I was just playing a bunch of video games every night," he told *Fortune* in 2019. "I was on academic probation, really trying to figure out what was going on and didn't understand why some days I would wake up and be able to go to class and then other days not. . . . I remember freshman year, I had a Spanish final, and I woke up in the morning, then like looked at my clock and just decided not to go to class and take my final. I ended up failing the course."[17]

> "I basically had less than a 2.0 GPA after two years of college because I was just playing a bunch of video games every night. I was on academic probation, really trying to figure out what was going on and didn't understand why some days I would wake up and be able to go to class and then other days not."[17]
>
> —*Psychiatrist and former gaming disorder sufferer Alok Kanojia*

Although many who suffer from gaming disorder are college aged, younger people can also develop this type of issue. Technology has made handheld video games a common gift for children, and many games for younger kids are even marketed as educational tools. The ubiquitous nature of video games in adolescent society has led many people to miss many of the signs of a problem. David Atkinson is a psychiatrist and associate professor at the University of Texas Southwestern. He says, "Parents look at these items as something they need to set limits on, but almost never as something that may become out of their and their child's control."[18]

Gaming disorder is more common in younger people, but many adults also suffer from this problem. Although the symptoms are the same regardless of age, they can present in slightly different ways for adults. Like kids, adults with gaming disorder spend excessive amounts of time playing, and they have a similar lack of control over that time. However, adults who have difficulty regulating their gaming may let their professional lives suffer, arriving late to work after long nights of play. They may skip important meetings or fail to complete vital projects on time. They may even get fired. They might also shirk personal responsibilities, such as picking up their kids from school or showing up to plans with friends.

ON THE OUTSIDE LOOKING IN

The first thing family members and friends might notice is the gamer's absence from communal activities. A person with this

Someone who is addicted to video games might choose video games over spending time with family and friends. As with other addictions, withdrawal symptoms may be experienced while limiting gameplay.

problem will prioritize video game time over almost everything else in his or her life—family meals, recreational activities, and even important celebrations. Gamers who have difficulty regulating their play may stay up all night playing a game but

Declining grades can be one result of gaming disorder. When parents notice, they may be upset with their child and try to change the behavior.

likely won't make time to go to the movies with friends or out to a restaurant for a loved one's birthday. They may cancel standing plans at a moment's notice or simply not show up.

They will likely become defensive when others show concern about all the time they are spending gaming, insisting that it is less than it appears or even lying about it. Loved ones may also notice that the gamer becomes highly distressed when access to gaming is limited or denied. A teenager whose parents take his gaming system away in an attempt to solve the problem, for example, may go to great lengths to avoid this punishment—bargaining to keep the device in his possession or finding ways to game even after being told that it is not allowed.

Parents may notice that their child who once studied hard and earned good grades now puts no effort into schoolwork. Grades typically suffer as a result. A teen experiencing gaming disorder will also avoid other responsibilities, such as household chores. Eventually, even time spent with friends can be sacrificed for more game time. Many problem gamers will also skip meals or stay up well past their normal bedtime as they strive to make it to the next level of their favorite video game. When these habits persist for at least twelve months, gaming disorder may be a serious problem. In a piece she wrote on the subject for *Parents*, journalist Maressa Brown concluded, "Basically, it can't be considered a diagnosis until the behavior has fully dominated the player's life."[19] However, it's not clear that games actually cause these problems. It's also often unclear whether gaming disorder is a symptom of an underlying problem, such as depression or anxiety.

> "Basically, it can't be considered a diagnosis until the behavior has fully dominated the player's life."[19]
>
> —*Journalist Maressa Brown*

DIAGNOSING GAMING DISORDER

The first step in getting help for gaming disorder is seeking a diagnosis from a qualified mental health professional. For people who have already been diagnosed with another mental illness, such as depression, an excellent place to start would be their current therapist's office. For those who do not currently have a mental health provider, an appointment with a family doctor is a good starting point. Primary care physicians can often conduct a basic assessment and then make a referral to a mental health specialist if necessary. Many insurance companies also require a referral of this sort in order to cover the related expenses.

As with many other mental health problems, there are no standard tests for gaming disorder, although researchers are working to develop them. Instead, a caregiver will look at the range of symptoms the patient is experiencing and evaluate the situation based on their quantity, intensity, and duration. The appointment might begin with a general discussion about the patient's preoccupation with gaming and how it has affected his or her life over the last year. The doctor may be particularly interested in how the patient responds when the game is taken away. Symptoms such as extreme anxiety, irritability, or sadness, for example, are often signs of withdrawal—the clinical term for the reaction an addicted person experiences when access to the addictive object or substance is removed.

Just because a person has not been diagnosed with depression or another mental health issue, it does not mean that one is not present. For this important reason, an evaluation for gaming disorder should include a thorough psychiatric assessment. The approach the caregiver uses to treat gaming disorder may differ depending on other problems the patient is facing.

Although the *DSM-5* does not yet recognize gaming disorder as an independent issue, the manual lists several symptoms that are likely to be present in someone with this problem. A person with gaming disorder will probably be thinking about gaming even when not playing video games—and

Who Can Diagnose Gaming Disorder?

Before gaming disorder can be treated, a licensed mental health care provider must diagnose the condition. Many different kinds of mental health professionals can perform an evaluation for gaming disorder. A gamer or a family member can make an appointment with a psychiatrist, a psychologist, or a therapist who treats the condition. No matter how certain someone may be that a person has gaming disorder, a formal diagnosis is essential to receiving proper treatment. Although many insurance companies do not acknowledge gaming disorder, the ones that do will only pay for treatment once the diagnosis has been made. Likewise, many specialists will only treat patients who have been formally diagnosed. If the patient suffers from another mental health problem for which medications may be necessary, a medical doctor such as a psychiatrist must write the prescription. The diagnosis of gaming disorder remains controversial. Some experts warn that focusing too much on gaming behaviors could distract therapists from underlying issues, such as depression, anxiety, or ADHD.

The *DSM-5* lists ten common symptoms of gaming disorders. Five of these must be present within the last year in order for someone to be diagnosed with the condition.

feeling sad or anxious when unable to game. A person with this problem may also spend an increasing amount of both time and money on the pastime. Even if the person wants to stop gaming, abstaining typically proves too difficult. Other hobbies and interests fall by the wayside as gaming becomes an all-consuming activity. Even when the gamer is aware that gaming has become an unhealthy obsession, gaming remains the most important priority. It is the gamer's go-to solution for improving a bad mood. When gaming time is threatened, the gamer might lie to loved ones to protect it, even if that means threatening relationships instead. School or work fails to matter more than the gaming, so people may drop out or get fired.

According to the *DSM*'s proposed criteria, a person who has experienced five or more of these symptoms within a year fits the general criteria for a diagnosis of gaming disorder, though the diagnosis remains unofficial. However, many scholars have critiqued some of these symptoms as problematic, and it's not difficult to see why. While some of the symptoms are clearly unhealthy, others are less definitive. Someone who enjoys gaming may understandably look forward to taking part in the activity, especially after a bad day. Playing games to relieve stress might even be a healthy choice, especially for young people with other mental health issues such as ADHD or depression. Katie Hurley is a licensed clinical social worker who works with young people and their families. She points out, "Children and adolescents already diagnosed with these disorders might seek out gaming to cope with emotions, connect with others, or feel successful."[20]

Many scholars are unhappy with these symptoms because they believe gaming is being treated differently from other hobbies. For example, they suggest replacing the word *gaming* with *sports* to demonstrate this. Athletes routinely think about their sport when not playing, would feel upset if they couldn't play, spend time and money on it, or give up other activities to play more. For some outcomes, such as reducing negative moods, experts believe hobbies that help reach that outcome are a positive thing. They say that there is little reason to believe using games this way is bad. Indeed, they argue that the evidence shows the symptoms associated with gaming disorder often do not distinguish between people who have actual problems versus those who are healthy but just enjoy games as a passionate hobby.

> "Children and adolescents already diagnosed with [ADHD and depression] might seek out gaming to cope with emotions, connect with others, or feel successful."[20]
>
> —*Licensed clinical social worker Katie Hurley*

Because gaming disorder is not yet listed as a diagnosis in the *DSM-5*, some mental health providers may be unwilling to use this term as an official diagnosis. Writer Anya Kamenetz addressed this issue in a 2019 article for National Public Radio. "Labeling someone an addict," she stated, "essentially saying he or she has a chronic disease, is a powerful move."[21] This

Some scholars point out that many people use video games in healthy ways. Families may play games together to relax and have fun.

does not mean that mental health professionals who prefer not to use the term *gaming disorder* cannot help a person who is struggling, however. Kamenetz pointed out that many caregivers can still treat the problem with a range of therapies.

CHAPTER THREE

What Is Life like with Gaming Disorder?

n the beginning, before the habit evolves into a bigger problem, gaming is simply a form of entertainment—a way to pass time or relax. Playing the games is fun, so the person continues the behavior. For kids, a video game habit is often made easier by adult family members. Video games and gaming systems are common gifts for children on birthdays and holidays. Many parents even use them as rewards for good behavior or high grades.

Soon, however, the fun may turn into difficulties regulating the play. In 2017, a twenty-seven-year-old man named Adam recalled how his spiral into gaming disorder began. He told the *Chicago Tribune* that he had played video games since he was

Those with video game addictions may not realize or admit they have a problem. They continue to play video games despite the impact it has on their relationships and health.

just three years old. His parents bought him educational games at this age, but as he got older, he played more and more games. "To be honest," his mother shared in the article, "the whole concept of video game addiction was very foreign. All we cared about was that the games would not be violent."[22] What she and her husband did not realize was just how much time Adam was spending playing. Little did they know, for instance, that as a teen he often set his alarm for the middle of the night so he could keep playing.

Adam was aware that he was spending too much time playing video games, but he wasn't ready to take the problem seriously. "I would joke with friends about sleep being the first to go, then schoolwork, then family and friends. It would just cut into those things as you needed more time."[23] As he got older, Adam knew that he had to do something, but he wasn't sure what that something was. He tried quitting the games on his own, a solution that proved difficult. He repeatedly uninstalled games only to reinstall them when he couldn't abstain from playing any longer.

"I would joke with friends about sleep being the first to go, then schoolwork, then family and friends. It would just cut into those things as you needed more time."[23]

—Adam, a young man with gaming disorder who preferred to omit his last name

What finally inspired Adam to give the games up for good was the risk of losing someone important to him. While dating a woman he cared about deeply, he resorted to lying to her one evening when they had plans. He made up a wild story about why he had to cancel. Later, feeling embarrassed and guilty, he admitted to her that he had created the fabrication so he could feed his gaming disorder. Scared of losing the relationship over his gaming problem, he finally gave up the video games for good. He changed his passwords to gibberish so he couldn't remember what they were, signed out of his accounts, and never looked back.

In most cases, issues with gaming regulation begin as something else, such as depression, stress, or anxiety. People turn to games because they are fun, and they can relieve negative moods. This can be a good thing in most cases. However, some people may have difficulty regulating their behavior and returning to less-pleasant life tasks. Gaming disorder rarely begins simply because someone spent too much time gaming. Even with anecdotes involving extreme cases, most individuals acknowledge the problems began with depression or other life issues.

The good news is that, unlike substance abuse, evidence suggests that most cases of gaming disorder are mild and go away by themselves without even requiring treatment. In some cases, a therapist may need to guide the family to assist with limit setting. Unlike with substance abuse, abstinence from gaming is rarely a desired outcome. Indeed, this comes with its own risks, such as cutting off youth from their social connections and stress relief. Rather, gaming time is typically made into a reward for completing other life requirements, such as homework and chores. In rare cases, more extensive therapy may be required or the impairments may cause wider problems to a player's health.

IRRESPONSIBLE BEHAVIORS

A man who asked to be called Ian shared his story about gaming disorder with the *Guardian*. Although his situation was extreme, it illustrates how a serious case of gaming disorder can spiral into a truly dangerous situation. Ian began by limiting his game time to the weekends, but even then he was showing signs of a disorder. He would sit down at his computer on Friday after work and essentially remain there until late Sunday night. He said he would only leave his chair to use the bathroom. When staying awake became too challenging for him, he resorted to taking amphetamines—drugs that act as stimulants in the body—to keep his eyes open.

Soon Ian was ignoring both his children and his professional responsibilities to fulfill his urge to game. Before he admitted that he needed help, he lost his family and his job because of his problem. Now in recovery for gaming disorder, he feels ashamed of his condition. "People look down on it," he told the *Guardian*. "They don't think of it as serious. But it's the same as gambling, alcohol, drugs, or any other addiction. It can be very dangerous, very harmful, and very destructive."[24]

Like Ian, some pathological gamers also fall into substance abuse. Tom Bissell was a successful writer when video games and drugs became dual addictions for him. "Soon I was sleeping in my clothes. Soon my hair was stiff and fragrantly unclean," he wrote in an article for the *Guardian* about both problems.[25] Soon, he also said, he was spending hundreds of dollars each week on cocaine to fuel his video game habit.

> "Soon I was sleeping in my clothes. Soon my hair was stiff and fragrantly unclean."[25]
>
> —Writer Tom Bissell, who developed gaming disorder

Addiction, regardless of the type, makes people suffering from it generally unreliable. Those who care about the person suffering may or may not understand this, but understanding does not necessarily translate to tolerance. Frequently, those closest to the person will ask him or her to seek help. Some even stage interventions, concerted efforts by family and friends to convince the person to get that help. In order for the intervention to be successful, though, the person with the problem must agree to seek treatment.

Thankfully, most cases of gaming disorder are not as serious as Ian's or Tom's, but for the small percentage of people who go down this kind of road alongside their pathological gaming, developing addictions and losing important relationships are

Gamers may turn to drugs to help them stay awake and alert while playing games for long periods of time. This makes it even more difficult to change gaming behavior.

real risks. Sometimes the situation gets much worse before it gets better.

Avoiding responsibilities at work and home is common among people with gaming disorder. Issues related to problematic gaming make it difficult to follow through with these commitments because all the gamer wants to do is keep gaming, and he or she will often do whatever it takes to make that happen—even if it means disappointing themselves or others. Problem gamers may start out by skipping homework assignments to make more time for gaming but in some cases may skip classes or entire days of school.

HOW GAMING DISORDER AFFECTS RELATIONSHIPS

Gaming disorder can damage a person's relationships. As some gamers withdraw from social routines to make more time for play, family members and friends may feel hurt or angry about being ignored, lied to, or stood up repeatedly. When confronted about these issues, the person may become irritated. The person may respond by pulling away even further.

While the gamer may choose to stop seeing friends who insist that gaming has become a problem, staying away from family members completely isn't quite as easy. A teen who lives at home, for example, typically encounters parents and siblings daily. Once family members have expressed concern about the gaming, however, these interactions are likely to become more stressful. The very nature of gaming disorder plays a role in this stress. The more a person plays video games, the more that stress from the games trickles over into the gamer's everyday life. After losing a battle or other challenge in the game, they will likely be even more on edge with the people around them.

Wesley Yin-Poole suffered from gaming disorder—and the effects it had on his relationships—for many years before he was ready to admit the problem. In a piece he wrote for Eurogamer, he recalled,

> I wasn't blind to what was happening. My family was on my back all of the time about my lifestyle, and my girlfriend . . . let's just say she wasn't happy either. My time with the game caused arguments, fights and every so often a slam the door moment. At the time, I didn't think I was addicted. . . . If someone had suggested it then, I would have laughed in their face. But now, over a decade later, I believe I was.[26]

The negative reactions that a person with gaming disorder directs toward family members can even prevent many concerned loved ones from broaching the topic, for fear that the person will become angry. Some parents try to deal with the problem by removing the computer or gaming system from the household, but many have found that this approach only elicits more intense negative reactions. In an interview with ABC News, parents Al and Christine shared their story about their son Josh's battle with gaming disorder. They confided that Josh became

Gaming disorders can have a negative impact on relationships. People who are addicted to video games may prioritize games over those they care about.

unreasonably angry when they withheld his video games. "When we did take it away," Christine said, "there was a lot of problems in our house with his behavior."[27] Sometimes Josh would even punch holes in their home's walls to express his discontent. Christine admitted that her son's reactions often frightened her.

Individual stories like these show the ugliest, worst-case scenarios of gaming disorder. Many times news media outlets feature these extreme stories because they grab viewers' attention. Some critics of gaming disorder even think the media features such extreme cases of gaming disorder for the purpose of attracting high ratings or internet traffic. If these stories are the worst news, though, the better news is that most people who suffer from gaming disorder won't go to the extremes that Wesley and Josh did before getting help. Discussing their struggles—however extreme or rare they might be—shows people just how dangerous pathological gaming can become.

Andrew Kinch founded the website GameAware to help people who love games as much as he does keep enjoying them without letting them become a problem in their lives. His website cautions, "Try not to fall into the two extreme points of view about video games. Games aren't harmless when they are played to excess, and they definitely aren't worthy of the fear mongering seen in sensationalized media."[28]

"Try not to fall into the two extreme points of view about video games. Games aren't harmless when they are played to excess, and they definitely aren't worthy of the fear mongering seen in sensationalized media."[28]

—GameAware website, which aims to help gamers find balance between gaming and the rest of their lives

GOING FOR BROKE

Like other behavioral overuse conditions, gaming disorder can lead a person down a dark and dangerous path. Those who don't have parents or someone else to help keep a roof over their heads can even

Parents may have payment information stored on devices. This allows children to easily make purchases on the app store and play games.

find themselves in dire financial circumstances as a result of their gaming problem. When addicted gamers lose their jobs as a result of poor work performance, or from not showing up at all, they often have a hard time keeping up with their rent,

Helping Someone with Gaming Disorder

Family and friends who are concerned that a loved one has developed gaming disorder usually want to help, but often they do not know where to start. Talking to the gamer is the most obvious first step, but if the problem has truly become a disorder, it can be difficult to get through to the person. Parents of younger gamers can set limits on gaming time or make appointments with a counselor to discuss whether gaming has become a disorder, but family members and friends of adult gamers cannot force them to seek help. It is vital for the people who love a problem gamer to understand that they cannot control his or her behavior. Until the person is ready to take responsibility for the problem, it is unlikely that the situation will change.

electric bill, and other living expenses. But they will do anything not to lose their internet connection and game subscriptions. In rare cases, they may overdraw their bank accounts or run up huge credit card debt so they can keep playing their video games. Some may even borrow or steal money from the people they love to keep up with their habits.

Even younger kids who have no financial responsibilities can become so dependent on playing video games that they resort to stealing. The amounts of this theft can add up to a considerable amount of money. Lorrine Marer, a behavioral specialist who treats gaming disorder, told journalists for Bloomberg, "Parents have lost substantial amounts of money by not paying attention to whether their credit card is tied to the game console."[29] Kids use their parents' card numbers to set up video game subscriptions without their permission, and unless the parents look over the itemized statement, they don't even realize it has happened. In this way gaming disorder is a lot like another type of behavioral addiction—gambling. Just as problem gamblers continue the cycle of gambling, more money just keeps the problem going.

CHAPTER FOUR

How Is Gaming Disorder Treated?

The biggest hurdle to treating gaming disorder is getting the person with the problem to accept that there is indeed a problem. Once a person takes this enormous step, he or she can move on to seeking treatment, which can also present a few obstacles. Because there is no clear consensus about the legitimacy of gaming disorder as a mental health disorder, there also is no standardized treatment method yet. Still, many caregivers have sought to develop effective treatment plans for gamers with this problem. Gamers seeking help, as well as their concerned loved ones, may have to do a bit of digging to find those caregivers, though.

When Sally Bracke's adult son Charlie told her that he thought he had a gaming problem in 2015, she was ready to do everything she could to help him get the care he needed. Her first challenge was finding a treatment facility that recognized

People may attend group therapy sessions to treat gaming disorder. They are able to get support from others who are going through a similar situation.

gaming disorder. After making numerous phone calls, Sally started losing hope. No one seemed to be willing to treat her son's problem.

She finally located a rehabilitation center in Washington State—far from where the family lived in Indiana—that treated gaming disorder. Shortly after arriving, Charlie felt confident that the trip had been worth the effort. "Just being around other people who had gone through what I had gone through and knew what it felt like made a huge difference," he told the *New York Times*. "I felt accepted. It almost sounds corny to say it, but I got there and immediately felt I had made the right choice."[30]

> "Just being around other people who had gone through what I had gone through and knew what it felt like made a huge difference. I felt accepted. It almost sounds corny to say it, but I got there and immediately felt I had made the right choice."[30]
>
> —Charlie Bracke, who underwent rehabilitation for gaming disorder

Another obstacle that the Brackes faced, however, was the high cost of treatment. Their insurance company refused to pay the bill, saying that it did not recognize gaming disorder as an official diagnosis. Sally and her husband ultimately took out a second mortgage on their house to pay for Charlie's forty-five day stay, which totaled $22,000. Although in-patient stays for virtually any type of mental health treatment can be expensive, it is important that people dealing with pathological gaming be careful when choosing a facility of this kind. Knowing that gaming disorder is still a controversial diagnosis that many doctors and hospitals do not yet treat, some disreputable treatment facilities charge inflated prices for so-called gaming disorder treatment with the objective of scamming people out of their hard-earned money. A reputable facility should not be offended if a patient asks for references or accreditations before entering treatment.

Today more insurance companies cover treatment for gaming disorder, but many still do not. Kristine Grow is a spokesperson for America's Health Insurance Plans, the national trade association that represents the health insurance community. In a 2018 interview with MarketWatch, she explained, "There are more studies that need to happen before gaming addiction makes its way into the *DSM-5*, which is a critical component before this begins to be covered under a lot of plans."[31]

> "There are more studies that need to happen before gaming addiction makes its way into the *DSM-5*, which is a critical component before this begins to be covered under a lot of plans."[31]
>
> —Kristine Grow, spokesperson for America's Health Insurance Plans

The fact that a stay at one rehabilitation center isn't covered by a particular insurance plan does not mean that the plan will not treat gaming disorder at all. Each insurer works a bit differently, but many companies will work with patients and caregivers to find a treatment plan that will work for all parties involved. Problem gamers who have another mental

Different Problem Behaviors, Different Treatments

Although some people compare gaming disorder to addictions to alcohol or drugs, there is a marked difference in the ways that these afflictions are treated. People who become dependent on substances must employ complete abstinence in order to manage their addictions successfully. Someone with alcoholism cannot learn how to have just a single drink, for example. Gaming disorder is more like food overuse. Since people need to eat to survive, people who habitually overeat must create a new relationship with food to manage their problematic use. The prevalence of computers and smartphones in everyday life makes it difficult, if not impossible, for problem gamers to avoid video games entirely. For this reason, mental health professionals who treat gaming disorder typically use treatment methods that teach problem gamers to create a new relationship with these devices. Although patients may be expected to go through a period of time without playing any games, electronics are usually reintroduced to them gradually and with clear limits that make moderation an easier task.

health diagnosis, such as depression or anxiety, often have the easiest time with this process, as there is a fair amount of overlap in the most common treatments for these disorders and gaming disorder.

EFFECTIVE TREATMENTS

Therapeutic techniques for treating gaming disorder, similar to those for depression, often begin with behavior modification, an approach frequently referred to in the mental health community as cognitive behavior therapy (CBT). A mental health practitioner, such as a psychologist or therapist, may start by helping the patient create a new schedule that limits game time. Since gaming disorder is a behavioral overuse disorder, a practitioner who specializes in problem behaviors may be the smartest choice. The new plan will likely also prioritize getting enough sleep, eating a healthy diet, getting enough exercise, and incorporating alternative forms of recreation into the patient's life.

Patients seeking to manage their gaming disorder will typically begin by meeting with a mental health provider for individual counseling or psychotherapy. Family sessions may be recommended if relationships with family members have been affected by the gamer's disorder. Often group therapy is also helpful for treating gaming disorder, as the support of others dealing with the same problem can be empowering for problem gamers.

The mental health provider will also suggest ways for dealing with the temptation to game longer than the agreed-upon period. "Healthy levels of gaming can quietly become problematic if left unchecked," notes licensed clinical social worker Katie Hurley.[32] In extreme cases, an inpatient stay may be necessary to break the gaming habit.

By 2019, clinical trials were underway to see whether medications might be helpful for treating gaming disorder. Many of these drugs have been created to inhibit the brain's reuptake of dopamine—effectively interrupting the pleasure

Cognitive behavioral therapy can be used to treat multiple mental illnesses, not just gaming disorder. CBT helps a person change their thoughts and behaviors so that they can be happier and healthier.

response that patients experience from gaming. For gamers

who also suffer from depression or another mental health issue

associated with gaming disorder, prescriptions used to treat that problem may be helpful for treating gaming disorder, too. Of course, the controversial nature of gaming disorder makes prescribing medication to treat it especially concerning to those who question the disorder's validity. Taking medication of any kind should only be done when that medication has been proven both safe and effective, and for gaming disorder, the jury will be out at least until clinical trials are completed.

Following the treatment plans provided by professional caregivers is a must for people with gaming disorder. They must remain committed to their plans for management of the disorder to be successful.

OTHER TREATMENTS IN DEVELOPMENT

The WHO's controversial classification of gaming addiction as a psychological disorder has led to numerous studies that aim to identify the best treatment methods for the problem. One such study, conducted in Germany, claimed a success rate of 70 percent. Notably, the approach outlined in this study did not utilize psychiatric drugs. Rather, it focused on education and self-awareness so that participants could play an active role in their own recovery. The biggest goal was to adjust their relationships with computers, the internet, and video games. Using diaries to record triggers that led to extended gaming, the patients expounded on how they felt prior to these binges.

The leaders of the study then taught them to redirect that energy into other behaviors.

Kai W. Müller, one of the authors of the study, wrote, "Modification of the relevant characteristics is the crucial aim of the intervention. This can for instance be enhancing the patient's resilience towards stressful events, or his or her social skills, understanding of his or her emotional responses and simultaneously developing alternative explanations and reactions."[33]

While the results of this study are promising, more research into the treatment method is needed to know whether it will be as successful for a wider group of people with gaming disorder. All 143 people who took part in Müller's study were men. While most people who seek treatment for gaming disorder are indeed men, women and younger people need help as well.

PREVENTION

As researchers work to find the best ways to treat gaming disorder, other mental health providers have begun focusing on ways to prevent gaming disorder. With gaming becoming more and more popular among young people, this approach could play an important part in reducing the number of people who suffer from gaming disorder in the future. It may be easier to prevent the problem than treat it.

A therapist may encourage the use of a diary to track moods and thoughts that lead to problem gaming. This allows someone with gaming disorder to evaluate what triggers their need for video games.

Gamers, parents, and other loved ones top the list of people who should be vigilant of how much time a gamer is spending in front of the screen, but even some video game makers are stepping up to prevent game time from getting out of control. Nintendo, for example, is just one of several companies that have

Many Nintendo games have built-in features reminding players to take breaks. These suggestions can help gamers keep track of time.

set up reminders within their games for players to take breaks. Some gaming systems also have parental control features that make it possible for parents to set customized time limits that suit the needs of their families.

Just as education and awareness are essential to the success of future treatments for gaming disorder, educating young people about the dangers of spending too much time gaming can help prevent many gamers from developing the problem in the first place. Most parents understand that setting time limits is a smart move, but talking to older kids about why these limits are important can also be helpful. One of the few things that most experts agree on is that games aren't going anywhere. Many also agree that some video games, particularly the educational variety, have value when played in moderation. Families should discuss that value as well as the importance of time management. As Jeffrey Knutson of Common Sense Education shared in an interview with *Education Week*, "There's potential for some great conversations to be started here."[34]

TREATING GAMING DISORDER IN THE FUTURE

The event that will likely affect gaming disorder treatment the most in the future is its potential inclusion in a new revision of the *DSM*. No one knows exactly when such a revision will be released or whether it will indeed classify gaming disorder as an official diagnosis.

Some mental health caregivers are concerned about the high number of self-diagnosed problem gamers who are trying a self-help approach to the problem. Game Quitters, an online support community for people struggling with problematic gaming, is one of the largest resources for such gamers.

Gamers can visit the group's website for information about dealing with gaming disorder. They can also make contact with other problem gamers. While many people find the camaraderie of this group setting helpful, it is not a replacement for professional help.

In November 2019, the United Kingdom's National Health Service opened its first center specializing in treating internet and gaming disorders. Weeks before the center even opened its doors, Dr. Henrietta Bowden-Jones told *Fortune*, "We are inundated. We have got sixty referrals already."[35]

THE FUTURE FOR THE GAMING DISORDER DIAGNOSIS

To say that gaming disorder is a controversial topic is an understatement. Many people, including many of the brightest minds in the world of mental health treatment, have strong opinions about whether the disorder should have been designated an official diagnosis by the WHO, and if it is included in the next edition of the *DSM* these disputes are likely to continue. As child and adolescent psychiatrist Victor Fornari notes, "When a new disorder is proposed, we need to see if it will survive the test of time."[36]

> "When a new disorder is proposed, we need to see if it will survive the test of time."[36]
>
> —*Child and adolescent psychiatrist Victor Fornari*

It is clear that the vast majority of gamers are using video games in a healthy way, but it's also clear that some people do truly struggle with pathological gaming. When a person is spending so much time in front of a video game screen that important responsibilities, relationships, and the individual's happiness become victims of that singular pastime, something must change for the sake of the person's general well-being. More research is being done on the nature of pathological gaming and the approaches to treating it, helping experts distinguish the differences between healthy and unhealthy gaming.

Source Notes

Introduction: When Gaming Gets Out of Control

1. Quoted in Mark Smith, "The Real-Life Story of a Computer Game Addict Who Played for up to 16 Hours a Day," *Wales Online*, July 30, 2019. www.walesonline.co.uk.

2. Quoted in Harley Tamplin, "Gamer Played So Much He Lost Welsh Accent as He Only Talked to Foreigners Online," *Metro*, August 23, 2018. https://metro.co.uk.

3. Quoted in Tamplin, "Gamer Played So Much He Lost Welsh Accent as He Only Talked to Foreigners Online."

4. Quoted in Tamplin, "Gamer Played So Much He Lost Welsh Accent as He Only Talked to Foreigners Online."

5. Jonathan D. Raskin, "Debate over Gaming Disorder Is Not All Fun and Games," *Psychology Today*, January 31, 2019. www.psychologytoday.com.

6. Meredith E. Gansner, "Gaming Addiction in ICD-11: Issues and Implications," *Psychiatric Times*, September 12, 2019. www.psychiatrictimes.com.

Chapter 1: What Is Gaming Disorder?

7. Tanya J. Peterson, "How Many Hours of Video Games Is Too Much?" *HealthyPlace*, July 19, 2018. www.healthyplace.com.

8. Joseph Knoop, "What Is Gaming Disorder, and Who's the Most at Risk?" *Daily Dot*, June 21, 2018. www.dailydot.com.

9. Quoted in Cameren Rogers, "WHO Calls 'Gaming Disorder' Mental Health Condition," *WedMD*, June 20, 2018. www.webmd.com.

10. Quoted in Elizabeth Armstrong Moore, "Study Finds Online Gamers Aren't Antisocial Basement Dwellers," *CNET*, March 28, 2014. www.cnet.com.

11. Caitlin Gibson, "The Next Level," *Washington Post*, December 7, 2016. www.washingtonpost.com.

12. Quoted in Tara Haelle, "Don't Hate the Player: Controversy over Gaming as Mental Disorder Levels Up," *Psychiatry Advisor*, February 1, 2019. www.psychiatryadvisor.com.

13. Quoted in Anya Kamenetz, "Is 'Gaming Disorder' an Illness? WHO Says Yes, Adding It to Its List of Diseases," *NPR*, May 28, 2019. www.npr.org.

14. Quoted in German Lopez, "Video Game Addiction Is Real, Rare, and Poorly Understood," *Vox*, December 6, 2018. www.vox.com.

15. Shannon Green, "Video Gaming Disorder Is a Disease? Sounds like Cultural Bias to Me," *Orlando Sentinel*, June 16, 2019. www.orlandosentinel.com.

Chapter 2: How Is Gaming Disorder Diagnosed?

16. Quoted in Charles Hymas, "Warning over Link Between Depression and Video Game Addiction After MRI Scan Shows Proof," *Telegraph*, July 31, 2018. www.telegraph.co.uk.

17. Quoted in Lisa Marie Segarra, "Video Game Addiction: These Are the Warning Signs to Look Out For," *Fortune*, July 11, 2019. www.fortune.com.

18. Quoted in "Video Game Addiction: When Is Gaming More than Just a Hobby?" *Children's Health*, 2020. www.childrens.com.

19. Maressa Brown, "Gaming Disorder Is Sending Kids to Emergency Rooms: Here Are the Warning Signs," *Parents*, n.d. www.parents.com.

20. Katie Hurley, "Does Your Child Have Internet Gaming Disorder?" *Psycom*, August 28, 2018. www.psycom.net.

21. Kamenetz, "Is 'Gaming Disorder' An Illness? WHO Says Yes, Adding It to Its List of Diseases."

Source Notes Continued

Chapter 3: What Is Life like With Gaming Disorder?

22. Quoted in John Keilman, "Are Video Games Addictive like Drugs, Gambling? Some Who've Struggled Say Yes," *Chicago Tribune*, May 30, 2017. www.chicagotribune.com.

23. Quoted in Keilman, "Are Video Games Addictive like Drugs, Gambling? Some Who've Struggled Say Yes."

24. Quoted in Emily Reynolds, "'It Consumed My Life': Inside a Gaming Addiction Treatment Centre," *Guardian*, June 18, 2018. www.theguardian.com.

25. Tom Bissell, "Video Games: The Addiction," *Guardian*, March 20, 2010. www.theguardian.com.

26. Wesley Yin-Poole, "It's Time to Stop Running from Game Addiction," *Eurogamer*, May 22, 2019. www.eurogamer.net.

27. Quoted in Eric M. Strauss, Denise Martinez-Ramundo, and Alexa Valiente, "Michigan Teen Who Skipped School to Play Video Games Goes Through Treatment in the Wilderness," *ABC News*, May 19, 2017. https://abcnews.go.com.

28. "Gaming Disorder: Why It's Easy to Misunderstand," *GameAware*, n.d. www.gameaware.com.

29. Quoted in Jef Feeley and Christopher Palmeri, "Fortnite Addiction Is Forcing Kids into Video-Game Rehab," *Bloomberg*, November 27, 2018. www.bloomberg.com.

Chapter 4: How Is Gaming Disorder Treated?

30. Quoted in Ferris Jabr, "Can You Really Be Addicted to Video Games?" *New York Times*, October 22, 2019. www.nytimes.com.

31. Quoted in "Videogame Addiction Is Now an Official Disorder—but Will Health Insurers Pay for It?" *MarketWatch*, June 24, 2018. www.marketwatch.com.

32. Hurley, "Does Your Child Have Internet Gaming Disorder?"

33. Quoted in "Researchers Find a Promising Treatment for Video Game Addiction," *Vice*, July 16, 2019. www.vice.com.

34. Quoted in Michelle Davis, "World Health Organization's New 'Gaming Disorder' Raises Questions About Role of Educational Games," *Education Week*, June 18, 2018. https://blogs.edweek.org.

35. Quoted in Phil Boucher, "The U.K.'s Public Health Center for Gaming Disorders Marks a New Era in Fighting Tech Addiction," *Fortune*, October 11, 2019. www.fortune.com.

36. Quoted in "WHO Calls 'Gaming Disorder' Mental Health Condition."

For Further Research

Books

Evan Amos, *The Game Console: A Photographic History from Atari to Xbox*. San Francisco, CA: No Starch Press, 2019.

P. J. Graham, *Video Game Addiction*. San Diego, CA: ReferencePoint Press, 2019.

Patricia D. Netzley, *Online Addiction*. San Diego, CA: ReferencePoint Press, 2017.

Bradley Steffens, *Addicted to Video Games*. San Diego, CA: ReferencePoint Press, 2019.

Amanda Vink, *The Dangers of Digital Addiction*. New York: Lucent Press, 2020.

Internet Sources

Ian Bogost, "Why Is There a 'Gaming Disorder' but No 'Smartphone Disorder?'" *Atlantic*, June 28, 2018. www.theatlantic.com.

Heather Newman, "Researchers Release New Test for Gaming Addiction," *Forbes*, May 31, 2019. www.forbes.com.

Alice Park, "Gaming Disorder Is Now an Official Medical Condition, According to the WHO," *Time*, May 29, 2019. www.time.com.

Websites

American Addiction Centers: Gaming Disorder
https://americanaddictioncenters.org
/video-gaming-addiction

The website of American Addiction Centers includes information about gaming disorder and how to treat it.

Game Quitters
https://gamequitters.com

The organization Game Quitters seeks to help people cut back on their gaming, find support from peers, and discover new hobbies.

World Health Organization: Gaming Disorder
www.who.int/features/qa/gaming-disorder/en

The World Health Organization's website includes the 11th Revision of the *International Classification of Diseases (ICD)*, which features gaming disorder as one of its entries.

Index

Index Continued

Image Credits

About the Author

Tammy Gagne has written dozens of books for both adults and children. Her recent titles include *Women in the Workplace* and *Dealing with Self-Injury Disorder*. She lives in northern New England with her husband, her son, and a menagerie of pets.